anythink

Bizarre Birds

by Sandra Horning
Scholastic Inc.

Photo Credits
Photos ©: cover main: Dirk Freder/iStockphoto; cover background: Totajla/iStockphoto; back cover: Barry Hatton/Thinkstock; egg throughout: Coprid/iStockphoto; 1: Carmelka/iStockphoto; 2-3: Tom Brakefield/Thinkstock; 4-5 main: Gaardman/iStockphoto; 5 inset: Flip De Nooyer/Minden Pictures/National Geographic Creative; 6-7 main: Kevin Elsby/FLPA/Science Source; 7 inset: Sergey Uryadnikov/Dreamstime; 8-9 main: gabriela schaufelberger/iStockphoto; 8 inset: Kesu01/Thinkstock; 10-11 main: Otto Plantema/Minden Pictures; 11 inset: Tim Laman/National Geographic Creative/Alamy Images; 12-13 main: Jayanand Govindaraj/Dreamstime; 12 inset: Zwilling330/Thinkstock; 14-15 main: Leopardinatree/Thinkstock; 15 inset: SerengetiLion/Thinkstock; 16-17 main: ca2hill/Thinkstock; 17 inset: Mbridger68/Dreamstime; 18-19 main: Craig Dingle/iStockphoto; 19 inset: Craig Dingle/iStockphoto; 20-21 main: abzerit/Thinkstock; 20 inset: pchoui/iStockphoto; 22-23 main: Dave Watts/Alamy Images; 23 inset: Mastamak/iStockphoto; 24 inset: kenowolfpack/Thinkstock; 24-25 main: kojihirano/Thinkstock; 26 inset: kajomyot/Thinkstock; 26-27 main: TheNatureWeb/iStockphoto; 28-29 main: EcoPic/iStockphoto; 29 inset: JohnCarnemolla/iStockphoto; 30-31 main: Rusty Dodson/iStockphoto; 31 inset: Barry Hatton/Thinkstock; 32: Totajla/iStockphoto.

Copyright © 2017 by Scholastic Inc.

The publisher does not have any control over and does not assume any responsibility for author or third-party websites or their content.

No part of this publication may be reproduced, stored in a retrieval system, or transmitted in any form or by any means, electronic, mechanical, photocopying, recording, or otherwise, without written permission of the publisher. For information regarding permission, write to Scholastic Inc., Attention: Permissions Department, 557 Broadway, New York, NY 10012.

Library of Congress Cataloging-in-Publication Data
Horning, Sandra, 1970– , author. Bizarre birds / by Sandra Horning.
New York, NY : Scholastic Inc., 2017. | Series: Scholastic reader level 2
LCCN 2016015595 | ISBN 9781338047257 (pbk.)
LCSH: Birds—Behavior—Juvenile literature. | Birds—Morphology—Juvenile literature.
LCC QL698.3 .H58 2017 | DDC 598—dc23 LC
record available at https://lccn.loc.gov/2016015595

10 9 8 7 6 5 4 3 2 1   17 18 19 20 21

Printed in the U.S.A.   40
First printing, March 2017
Book design by Maeve Norton

All birds are related to one another, but they can be very different. All birds have wings, but not all of them can fly. Some birds are the size of your finger, while others are bigger than you are! Their feathers come in every color of the rainbow. Many birds make strange sounds and have other strange **behaviors**, too. These bizarre birds live all over the world!

Hoatzin

These South American birds smell like cow poop because they **digest** their food the same way that cows do. That's why many people call hoatzins "stink birds"! Hoatzins spend most of their time in swampy, wet areas and build their nests high up in the trees.

Hoatzin chicks are born with claws on their wings. These claws help the babies climb in and out of their nests until they can fly.

Bee Hummingbird

The bee hummingbird lives in Cuba, and it is the smallest bird in the world. It is only as long as a thumb! Spotting this tiny bird is like finding a treasure. When it is moving, its green and blue feathers shimmer. That is because the bee hummingbird's wings move so fast, human eyes see only a blur.

These birds can flap their wings 80 times in one second!

Shoebill

This giant stork-like bird can grow to be up to five feet tall. That's almost as tall as a full-grown human! The shoebill lives in east-central Africa. It feeds at night, eating fish, snakes, rats, and even baby crocodiles. No wonder it needs such a big beak!

The shoebill gets its name from its giant beak—it's about the size of an adult's shoe!

Ribbon-Tailed Bird of Paradise

Birds of paradise are some of the world's most beautiful birds. The ribbon-tailed birds of paradise are found in Papua New Guinea. They are known for their long tail feathers.

Why do they have such long tails? The tails help the male birds of paradise attract a **mate**. The males dance and display their feathers. They may even hang upside down. Now, that's bizarre behavior!

Some of the males have feathers almost as long as baseball bats!

Greater Flamingo

This pink bird is found in parts of Africa, the Middle East, and even Asia. The greater flamingo's long neck helps it find food in the warm, shallow waters where it lives. The flamingo's pink color comes from the **pigments** found in the food it eats. Shrimp is the greater flamingo's favorite meal. If a flamingo looks white, it probably isn't eating enough shrimp!

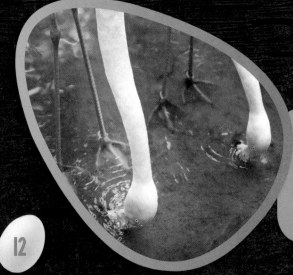

A greater flamingo can eat with its head upside down underwater!

Oxpecker

This African bird lives on top of animals such as rhinos, buffaloes, and giraffes. The oxpecker eats ticks, lice, worms, and other bugs off the host animal's hair and skin. Oxpeckers also eat earwax from the animals! Earwax is a good source of **nutrients** and energy—that may be why these bizarre birds eat it.

Oxpeckers even feed on animal blood!

Long-Eared Owl

This North American owl gets its name from the long **tufts** of feathers on either side of its head. The tufts look like ears. But this owl's ears are actually near the sides of its eyes. The long-eared owl has excellent hearing that helps it hunt in the dark. It can catch a tiny mouse using only its sense of sound.

The long-eared owl's super-quiet wings also help it sneak up on its prey!

Lyrebird

This Australian songbird can **mimic** a wide range of sounds. One lyrebird was recorded making car alarm and chainsaw sounds! The male with the best sounds, dances, and feathers attracts the most females to be its mate.

When this bird's tail feathers are open, they look like a musical instrument called a **lyre**. That's how it got its name.

Atlantic Puffin

The Atlantic puffin spends most of its life in the northern Atlantic Ocean. Good thing it is an excellent swimmer! This bird can dive as deep as 200 feet. That's more than half the length of a football field! The puffin uses its wings to fly, too. It can fly up to 55 miles per hour. That's as fast as a car travels on most highways!

The puffin uses its wings to stroke underwater to catch fish and other food from the sea.

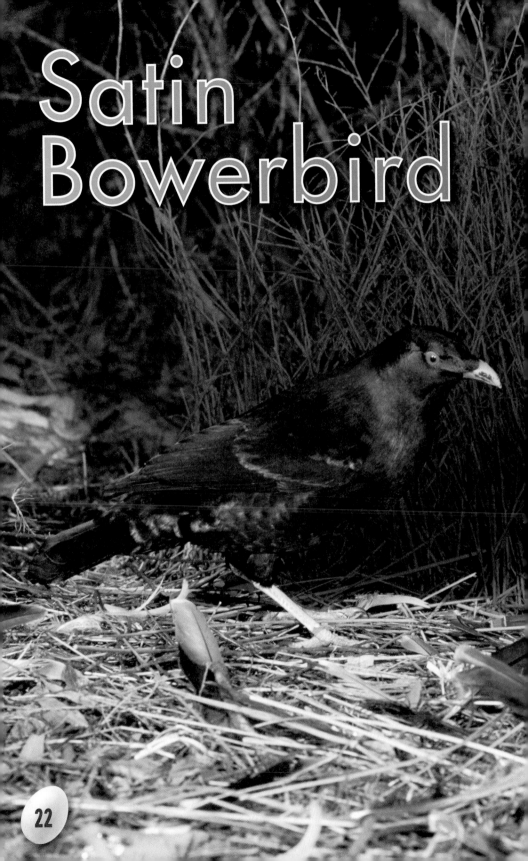

Satin Bowerbird

This Australian bird is an amazing artist! Instead of using fancy feathers to attract a mate, the male bowerbird builds a small hut made of sticks, called a bower. Then he decorates the bower with flowers, mushrooms, shells, and other objects. Some males add shiny objects, such as tinfoil or bottle caps. Some even kill bugs to use in their displays! The females are attracted to the best nests.

Sometimes a male uses only one color to decorate his bower.

California Condor

The California condor is the largest bird in North America. The condor is a type of vulture. These birds eat the bodies of dead animals. In the 1980s, the California condor was almost **extinct**. Only a few were left in zoos. But now, thanks to **conservation** efforts, there are more than two hundred of them living in the wild.

A condor's **wingspan** can be up to ten feet wide—that's twice as wide as a small car!

Common Tailorbird

This bird found in southern Asia can sew! The female tailorbird gathers green leaves and pokes holes in them with her bill. She finds spiderwebs or thin strips of plant to use as thread. Then she sews the leaves together using her beak as a needle. She leaves a small hole at the top. Inside, the tailorbird weaves a tiny nest for her eggs. What a talented little bird!

The common tailorbird is small enough to fit in the palm of your hand.

Ostrich

The ostrich—found in Africa—is the world's largest bird. It can stand up to nine feet tall and weigh as much as 285 pounds. That's bigger than the average man! The ostrich's wings are too small to lift its heavy body. Instead of flying, the ostrich runs very fast. All that running makes an ostrich's legs very strong. An ostrich can keep a predator away with one powerful kick!

Ostriches can reach speeds up to 43 miles per hour!

29

Tawny Frogmouth

This Australian bird is named for its strange beak that looks a lot like a frog's mouth! The tawny frogmouth looks a little like an owl, too. But this bird isn't part of the frog or owl families. At night, the tawny frogmouth eats insects, slugs, frogs, reptiles, and even other birds.

During the day, the **tawny** color of its feathers helps this bird blend in with the trees where it lives.

Glossary

behavior: the way a person or animal acts

conservation: the protection of animals and plants and their habitats

digest: to break down food in the stomach for the body to use

extinct: no longer found alive

lyre: a small harp-like instrument

mate: the male or female partner in a pair of animals

mimic: to copy someone or something else

nutrients: foods or other substances, like a protein or vitamin, that living things need to grow and live

pigments: substances that give color to something

tawny: a brownish-orange color

tufts: a bunch of hair, grass, or feathers attached at the bottom

wingspan: the distance from the tip of one wing to the other